Fighting With Myself

The Healing Power of Poetry

**by
Yvonne Glasgow**

Fighting With Myself

ISBN-13: 978-1546607427
ISBN-10: 1546607420

© 2017 Yvonne Glasgow

All rights reserved. No part of this book may be reproduced or transmitted in any form or by any means whatsoever without express written permission from the author, except in the case of brief quotations embodied in critical articles and reviews.

All photos were taken by and are the property of the author.

This book is dedicated to Dale Wicks, for being the one to remind me that love is possible and that hearts don't always have to get broken; his friendship and love make me feel like anything is possible.

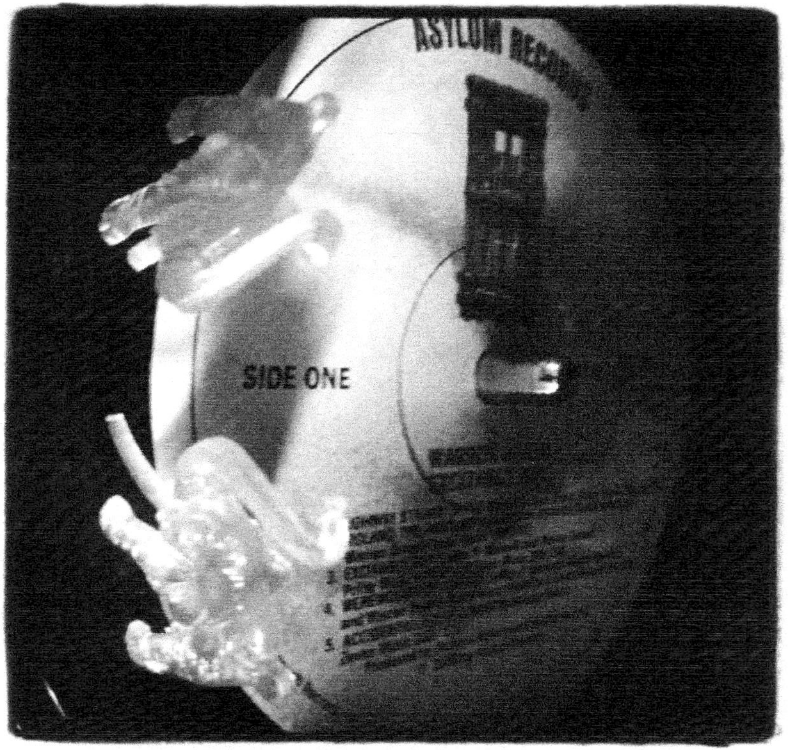
SIDE ONE

Table of Contents

- Preface
- Son of Abyss
- Goodbye, Friend. We've Grown Apart. Well, One Of Us Grew, Anyway.
- Some People Love A Lie
- My Positivity Poem
- I Hate Depression
- The Longest Hour/That Tomorrow
- The Things I left Behind
- In My Hatred, I'll Find Forgiveness
- Visions Of Who I Am
- This Is Anxiety
- I'm Over It
- Me Again
- The Dreaming Road
- Goodnight, Farewell
- Crashing And Burning
- Reaching Toward The Abyss
- My Fairy Tale
- What Is This Sleep You Speak Of?
- Where Am I Going?
- You
- You're The Sign
- Longing For Those Words
- Off Track
- Alone
- It's Over Now
- June Six Twenty-Fourteen
- Afterword
- About The Author

Preface

You live, you love, you get your heart broken, and then you move on and do it all over again. That's the way of life and love. We wonder, constantly, "If I told you I loved you, what would you say?". We worry and fret. We drive ourselves crazy over feelings for other people that may or may not feel the same way about us, ever. Sometimes we get into the wrong relationships, sometimes we even marry the wrong people altogether.

These things don't just happen in our romantic relationships either. Friendships can fall apart and so can family bonds.

Like many poets, my poetry is most often inspired by my life, and by my feelings. I write best, I believe, when my life is in turmoil. Sometimes I only get a sentence or two down though. Like, "I hate when I feel like my happiness is a lie, It never seems to matter how much I try." And then those lines just sit there wishing that the inspiration that started them would come back to finish them. Then there are times where I simply feel like I never want to stop writing and write a long poem, or numerous, somewhat related, poems in a row.

I have, "Dreams in my head and words in my heart," and they don't always make it onto the page, and they aren't always fully formed thoughts. If you're a writer of any kind, from lyrics to short stories, you can probably understand that. It's not writer's block because I don't believe in that fairy tale. It may just be my overly busy anxiety ridden mind that's always onto the next thought process or project before the last one is completed. I think all people that are truly blessed with creative talent experience this.

I also want to point out that not all of my poems are about love in the romantic sense. Broken friendships, family turmoil, and other life events often push those poetic words from my lips or my fingers. It's a way to deal with issues, to get those feelings out of my head, and a way to help me move on and find comfort and happiness again.

This book is full of poetry about love and loss. There are poems about friends that treated me wrong, about relationships that went sour and poems that are simply about the struggles of life in general. I am taking the time, as this book writes itself, to rewrite some of those poems that never found their finish, that only started as a sentence or two. I want them to have their story told too before it's time for these words to find their place in the world.

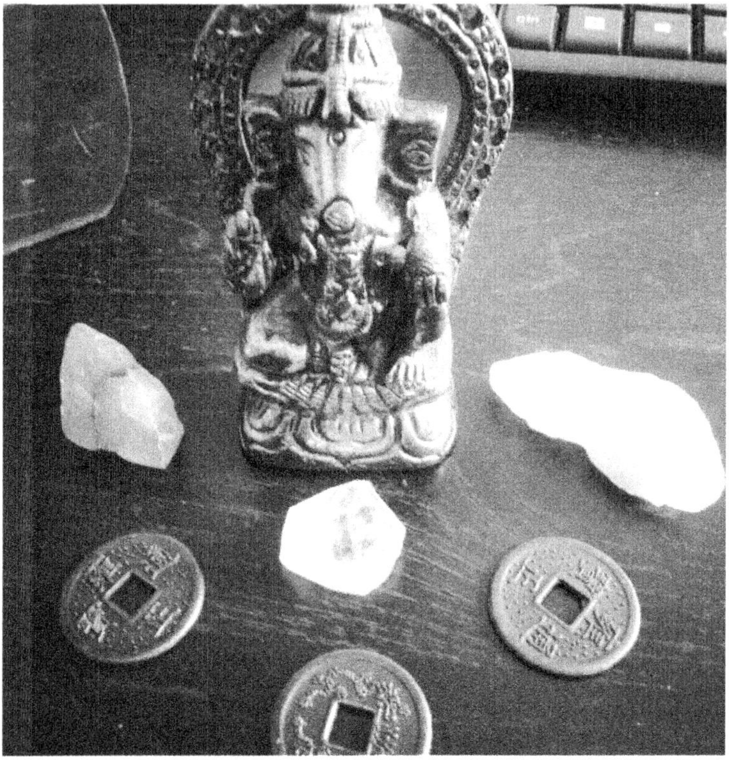

The Poems

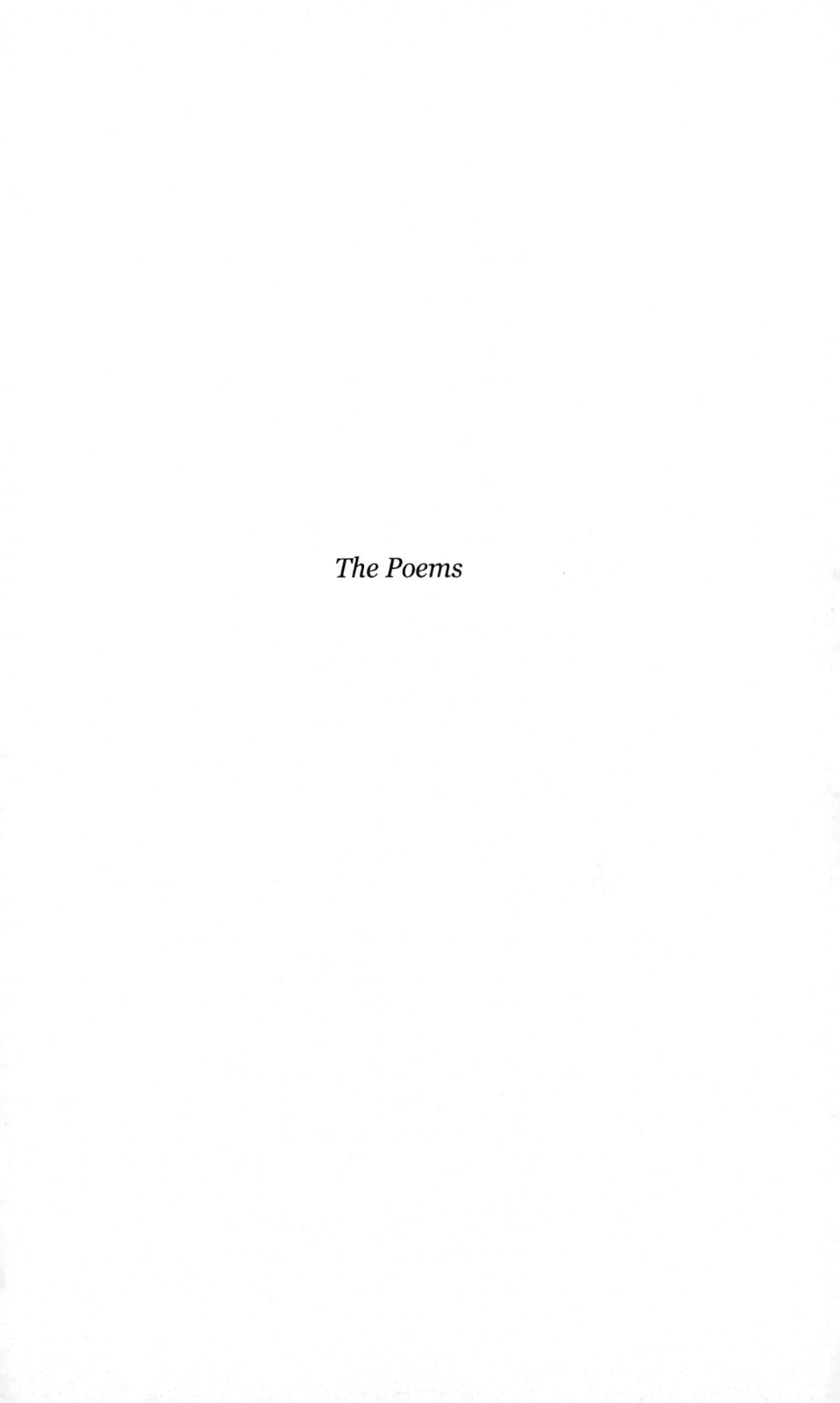

Son of Abyss

I'm falling into the abyss.
I need to quit thinking anyone actually cares.
Oh, you'll say you do,
But that's only when it's convenient for you.

You say you're there if I need you
But you're never around.
All I hear is the empty sound
Of my own beating heart.
Don't you start
To say that it's all going to be OK
Unless you can show me some kind of proof.

It will always be this way,
Nothing will ever really change.
You may think it's strange
But I'm getting used to it.
It's never going to quit,
The endless feeling of emptiness.

I'm falling into the abyss.
I need to quit thinking anyone actually cares.
Oh, you'll say you do,
But that's only when it's convenient for you.

I can't see the bottom,
Is there even one?
I'm pretty sure that I am done
Allowing you to fool me
Because now I can see
You're just no good for me.

Don't bother checking in on me,
The bottom, the abyss, is where I'll be.

About *Son Of Abyss*

I started this poem in February of 2017 when I realized the one "close" friendship I still had was going to fall apart when I realized it was a one-sided thing where I was continually there for her, but when I needed her all I got was arguments and resentment. While the main idea behind this poem was about friends that are only in the friendship for themselves, I feel like it could also be about anyone, from romantic partners to family members, that are too busy getting lost in their own heads to realize when they are hurting the people around them.

Goodbye, Friend. We've Grown Apart. Well, One Of Us Grew, Anyway.

Should I never change?
Always stay the same.
Never bending,
Never blowing in the wind.
Is it a sin
To grow from within?
Is it wrong to want to learn
To continue to yearn
For things that are new and different?

A chameleon only changes colors.
It does not change on the inside.
In my growth, I take pride
That I can continue to be
Someone new, to you and me.
Never growing stagnant in the waters
Living like the squatters
Like those that never change are bound to do.

If we all just stay the same,
Never learning, never growing
There will be no one knowing
How to create new things
How to live our dreams.
I am not the bad one
For not wanting to be done,
Not ending my journey in contentment.

I will never be content.
I always want to want more
To continue to explore
To take pride in change
And continue to rearrange.
My thoughts and my actions are not in stone.

> And I'd rather be alone
> Then share my success with you.

About *Goodbye, Friend. We've Grown Apart. Well, One Of Us Grew, Anyway.*

Sometimes a poem is simply obvious. To the person this one is about, it would be obvious. It was in direct retaliation to poetry written, angrily, about me. I think I responded eloquently. Of course, this book is the first time any eyes have seen this poem aside from mine. I'm not the dramatic type and I hate confrontation. To me, it's healthier to deal with your pain and anger in a creative and healing way.

Some People Love A Lie

You don't know what love is
I can honestly tell you this
People that love do not purposely cause pain
They are there for others when it starts to rain
When those dark clouds roll in
When they fall from grace again

You don't know this "love" act
Because it's something you lack
You lack the ability to have empathy
And those that loved you, you could not see
You put on blinders and hid away
Until they left you one day

When someone walks away
When someone closes a door
There's always a reason for
Their actions and their passion
When someone walks away
It's because they couldn't stay

You don't know how to love
You think it's just a shove
Something you can force on someone
And that's all you've done
No give, just take
That's what makes you fake

Because you didn't really love
You were too busy above
Looking down at people like insects
Instead of showing respect
And now you're alone
Stuck inside your hell of a home

About *Some People Love A Lie*

This poem is about a few people that have come and gone from my life. It's a poem about narcissists and sociopaths, at its core. It's about the fact that you can walk away from those people and move on in your life, and be happy without those types of people bringing you down constantly.

It's about understanding that we are all responsible for our own lives and we shouldn't expect other people to make us happy if we can't make ourselves happy. This poem is about so much, but most of all it was about me healing after a rough year, from leaving my ex-husband to realizing that the people I thought were my closest friends were not my friends at all. It was about realizing that people will continue to use you if you let them.

My Positivity Poem

Save yourself
Nobody else can save you
It's something you need to learn
If you never want to be blue

Take a negative day
And push the fear and pain away
You can give it a positive spin
It's all about the mood you're in

If you don't believe
If it's too hard to conceive
Let me be your proof
That it's all about your attitude

When you're positive more than not
You'll find there's a lot more you got
That's good in your day
You'll want to give some of that happiness away

Spread it with a smile
Talk to someone a while
Post a positive quote
Leave a friend a loving note

If you can't brighten your day
You'll chase everyone away
That's why I chose my attitude
To be one of only gratitude

I am thankful to be alive
That's something I don't hide
If my happiness is too much
I'm sorry about your luck

Don't give your dreams away
They'll come true one day
Just keep wishing and hoping
And avoid the ones that are moping

Just like a smile is contagious
Some anger rubs off in stages
You'll be blue a while
Then you'll be ready to cry

So don't give another that power
You don't need to be sour
Just think of positive things
And listen as your heart sings!

About *My Positivity Poem*

See, not all of my poetry is about broken hearts and bad friends. Sometimes it's positive. Of course, I did write this following one of those times of turmoil. It helped me to remember that silver lining still exists, and I am hoping that reading it in the midst of all of this depression and anxiety-laced poetry it will help you find some joy and happiness too.

I Hate Depression

When those voices in your head
Change from a whisper to a scream
And you can no longer ignore them.
You start to only dream
That things could ever get better.
It doesn't matter how good it is,
How good it was,
How good it could be,
Things can always end, die, go bad...
And they always will, won't they?

Depression
It inhales and exhales
Then chokes off the breath
It strangles and curses
And bleeds you to death
It piles boulders on top
It starts fires below
You'll be kicking and screaming
But it won't let you go
For a moment the sun shines
And you start to feel free
Then it blinds you and binds you
And you know it will never leave.

Waiting for the other shoe to drop
Or maybe I'll throw it at myself.
I make these things happen.
I am the common thread.
Sometimes I wish I was dead.
Doesn't everyone?
This life weighs a ton,
And I'm tired of carrying it on my shoulders.
I'll never stop getting older,
Until it's all over.

But depression,
It never ends.
It takes away your breath
It breaks and it bends.
It makes you curse and cower
Until you fear everything
Your own shadow will make you scream
And you try to hide
The whole time screaming inside
Knowing it will never let you go

Then,
For a moment the sun shines
And you start to feel free
But it finds you
And then blinds you and binds you
And you know it will never leave.

About *I Hate Depression*

The title is simple and yet speaks volumes to my relationship with depression. I hate it. I hate how it creeps up out of nowhere and it can steal away all of your happiness and joy. I hate that it can come in at any moment, even when you think your life is all puppies and rainbows.

This was originally two different poems, but as I was going through all my short little bits and pieces of words I saw a way that they could fit together and become more as a team.

The Longest Hour/That Tomorrow

That last hour, before my whole life changed
I thought about so many things
Like the changes of the world
as it turns.
I sat here, across from you, my nerves on edge
That panic attack continually creeping in
Knowing this was for the best
Knowing my life would be better that tomorrow

I knew why I was leaving
I knew it was the only way
I had to get my life back
It had to happen some day

But knowing didn't make it any less scary
Knowing I had to leave
It didn't make it any less frightening
Knowing my life would be better that tomorrow

When the longest hour was upon me
All I could do was wait
Staring at the computer screen
Anxiously trying not to grate
My teeth on edge, falling from the ledge
I fought the panic attack. A warning about tempting fate
But, my life was better that tomorrow

Without you...

I moved on
I learned to get along
It wasn't easy
But nothing ever is
It was for the best

> And I passed the test
> That let me find that tomorrow
> Instead of losing myself forever
> In your never ending sorrow.

About *The Longest Hour/That Tomorrow*

This poem was originally only titled The Longest Hour and was about half as long. I wrote it while I sat across the table from my ex-husband on the day I was to leave him. I was on the continual verge of a panic attack, worried he'd find out my plan and thwart it. I was scared of his angry side, scared of what physical harm would come to me. See, he never hit me, but he claimed to want to, many times. He was emotionally abusive though, and how many steps are there really between emotional abuse and physical abuse?

The Things I Left Behind

When I walked away, it was because I couldn't stay
(You pushed me away)
So many years of heartbreak, lead to a heart of stone
(Your heart, that is)
No more love have I known, not in this home
(Did you ever love me?
Was this ever real?
Or did you simply keep me around
So alone you wouldn't feel?)

The things I left behind are many
(The only one that mattered was you)
But one thing I took with me was my heart
(It's not yours anymore,
There is no room for you here)
My soul and my faith were intact, the day I left
(I took them back as well.
You don't deserve these things,
Your selfishness is all you get)

I left behind some heirlooms when I remembered items don't matter
It's what is in your head and heart that stay with you through the years (forever)
I left behind something in every room, but those things aren't me
What I took with me was the hope that I would recover
(And I have, as anyone can see)

For years I have been turned into another
(Someone I didn't even know)
All I wanted back was the person I suddenly lack
(And I found her hiding far below)
What I left behind, those things won't long stay on my mind

It's what I'm moving toward that matters to me
To once again feel what it's like to be free (I'm free)

I don't care about the things I left behind
You can burn them, give or throw them away
They are nothing but a hurtful and painful past to me
Because...

Without them, I can be free
Without you, I can be me.

About *The Things I Left Behind*

When you pack up and leave your life behind it can be a pretty traumatic experience, even if it's the best thing for you. I used poetry to deal with leaving my ex-husband. It was seriously one of the only things that got me through that first few months. Poetry and art, because, in all honesty, the main friends I thought I was coming "home" to were basically fair weather friends or users at best. The ones that claimed to be such good friends to me, and would always be there, and then turned their backs after I gave them the shirt off mine.

Friends come and go throughout our lives. But sooner or later you learn who the real ones are.

In My Hatred, I'll Find Forgiveness

My thoughts, when they involve you,
Are all about hatred and pain.
All the shit you put me through,
I refuse to ever do this again.
My heart is aching my brain is fried.
So many times I have tried,
I tried to love you and make you see
That whatever you want the world to be
You need to see it in order to make it so
But all you did is laugh at me,
Call my beliefs crazy, continuing to live in your misery.
Moments to anger, I'm afraid to speak,
I don't have the answers you seek,
So you take it out on me in harsh words.
And now I am leaving…

When I am gone I know I'll find
The strength to forgive you.
Because although you tried
You did not break my pride.
I know I deserve better than you.
Someday you'll forgive me too,
For walking away and leaving you alone.
But it was no one's fault but your own.

I never really hated you,
Although your love was always a lie.
For each day you wished to die,
I stood there by your side.
You had no will to live.
And I was never a blessing you counted.
This is to what our relationship amounted.
It was nothing.
It was garbage.
When you bond with someone in constant misery

> There is no way to really be free
> Without running far, far away
> And never looking back,
> Not even today.

About *In My Hatred, I'll Find Forgiveness*

This was another poem I wrote about the ex-husband (it's obvious, right?). Poetry, journaling, writing of any kind is a great way to work through the problems in your life, so don't look down on anyone that writes poetry about the things they have been through or are going through (as long as it's well written and they are using it as a lesson and not just as a way to bash someone else). It's therapy. I added the last section to this poem more recently, but it would have originally been written in March of 2016 (I left on March 4).

Visions Of Who I Am

I am looking at myself from some else's mind.
Will their opinion be kind?
My eyes don't know what they see anymore.
Who is that in the mirror?
Who am I?
Am I a loner?
Am I a survivor?
Am I a lover?
Am I a friend?
...Am I loved?

I was a wife, but I feel alone now.
I walked away one day.
But I don't miss a thing from the life I left behind.
What is life?
A series of events,
both good and bad,
that we are forced to have.
Forced to have unless you take it,
Or unless it's taken from you.

My life is a roller coaster.
Each time I exit the ride,
I find myself in another line.
No more lies.
I just want to enjoy life again.
Dream again.
Be me... Again.
Who am I?

I faced the day today
I could no longer run away,
From who I am, who I was?
I saw a need for strength
To embrace the things I kept at length

(That me I left behind)
A dreamer's dreams don't come true
(But they do)
And without them who are you?

Be the one that saves yourself,
Don't put your heart on that shelf.
Find that you that makes you smile
Even if it's been a while.
You are the hero of your own story,
You can end this life with some glory.
But you must understand,
You can't be a hero
Without, sometimes, looking like a zero.

About *Visions Of Who I Am*

This is another mix-up of a couple different poems. I Am My Own Hero was one of them, and rounded out the ending of this other one nicely, solving the problem of figuring out who I am. It took a lot of learning for me to finally realize that it doesn't make me a narcissist to understand that I am numero uno. If you don't put yourself first then no one else is really going to respect you. But you need to also understand there is a fine line between loving yourself and being conceited, and a fine line between caring for yourself first and not caring a thing about others. I'm the type that cares too much for everyone else, often neglecting myself.

This Is Anxiety

Grasping at straws
(Don't grab the short one)
Trying to pull you in
But silence is all you give
Anxiety thickens
(It's a killer)
I can't think straight
I worry that all I am doing
Is pushing you away
(It's irrational, I know)
It's my mind that's in control
I have no say
All I can do is hope
Have faith that you will stay
(Or that I won't push you away)
It keeps me awake at night
Whenever I'm alone
I feel like before I know it
One day you'll be gone
(But for now, you're still here)
I don't deserve love
(I know I do,
But this is how anxiety gets you)
I am used to only hate
('I love you' rang false from so many in the past)
The things in my life
Always turn sour
It's fate that you'll walk away
(But you're still here today)
So here I sit
Always waiting for the other shoe
I know it will drop
(I wait, and it doesn't,
But I'm always on the edge)
And someday I won't have you

(But that day hasn't come yet)
And nothing you can say
Seems to make a difference
Actions always speak the loudest
(And your actions say you care)
And sometimes they shout
But sometimes they seem silent
(My anxiety blocks them out)
And I feel alone
Wondering why I bother
To hope for something good...

About *This Is Anxiety*

This is one of those poems that could have been written about any relationship I've ever been in, friendship or romantic. Anxiety is one of those things that swallows you whole and you have no way to stop it. It's filled with irrational fears and they can creep up anytime, anywhere. Basically, you just hope you get through the panic attacks without chasing everyone in your life away!

I'm Over It

You broke me down into pieces
You couldn't give good enough reasons
For shattering my heart like a glass
Was like any normal daily task
You thought nothing of what you were doing to me
Only thinking of how good it would be
To have someone at your beck and call
Did you ever really care at all?

You swept me away
Caring only for yourself day to day
I should have known it couldn't last
Something from so far in the past
And you left me to blow away like dust
Leaving you was a must

Now I have no tears left for you
Walking away was the best thing to do
Moving on was an easy thing
And away from your negativity my heart can sing
It's strange to walk away
From something that always made you stay
But it was for a better change
Though in the beginning, it was strange

I've moved on so very far
So far, I don't care where you are
My life is better without you in it
Loving you was the best thing I ever quit
So now I've gotten over you
I've found I have better things to do
Like enjoy life and smile again
There were so many things to gain
Like my sanity and my happiness
And I'm over all your crappiness

I'm over the way you treated me bad
I am sure somewhere in your head you were glad
That I chose to leave
So you could blame me for the deceive
Instead of accepting your responsibility
Because you are just as guilty.

About *I'm Over It*

When you leave a long term relationship, this one being a straight and steady 8 ½ years, and an on-and-off-again 16 years prior to that, it takes a lot to get over it. Some people never do. Some people simply stay single when something that long-lasting doesn't actually last. I moved on immediately, but I still had issues in my head to work through and these poems helped me.

You see, I was in an emotionally abusive relationship and I spent a lot of that 8 plus years being brainwashed by a narcissist into believing I was worthless and a completely different person than I actually was. Even my sister pointed out, after I got the guts to leave, that she had seen me completely change, and not for the better. Poetry helped me work through the traces left of that "pod" Yvonne and find the real me again.

Me Again

I walked alone
Many years I've roamed
Looking for a place
I could finally call home
Home is where the heart is
But it's black and charred and wasted
When was the last time I tasted
Love that was actually true?
I never felt that with you
You know who you are
The one I left behind
So that I could again find
The woman deep inside
That spent years trying to hide
From hateful words and glances
Always playing games and dances
Never straight forward
Honesty was lacking
And that's what sent me packing.

I've found me again
I'll never lose her again
No one can change the wildling in me
I need someone that can see
My darkness is my light
And gives me my creative sight.

I fell one day
And there I lay
Finding comfort in the cold on the floor
But I knew soon I'd have to open the door
I stayed too long until things got old
And my heart grew cold
Then it was finally time to go away
No longer could I stay

Now I'm standing
My life again expanding
Though I trip and fall
I get up and stand tall
And the person who knocked me down
Is the one that looks like a clown.

And I was able to find me again
That girl from way back when
And no one will ever change me
I found someone that can see
My darkness is my light
And gives me my creative sight.

About *Me Again*

This is where I was finally able to accept that I didn't have to be what I had been turned into over those years. I could be a combination of the person I was before then and someone new that still remembered all of those lessons she learned.

The Dreaming Road

Asleep at the wheel
I can only feel
The cold dead hands upon me
I can no longer see
Since I am in a dream
But I feel it creep up on me

The dreaming road
As I behold
Is something filled with nightmares
A home for many scares
Sometimes they're hard to wake up from

I can't wake up from this dreaming road
Oh the nightmares I'll behold
Demons screaming, I can't awake
Ask god, before I die, my soul to take

I can't wake up from this dreaming road
Oh the nightmares I'll behold
Demons screaming, I can't awake
Ask god, before I die, my soul to take

The dreaming road
It leads me home
The place I can't be alone
If I wake
If I wake
Wake me before it takes me
Down the dreaming road again

If I go back
If the road takes me
The dreams will be nightmares
My life is already full of scares

So wake me now
Before it's too late
Or the dreaming road with forever be my fate.

About *The Dreaming Road*

Sometimes I like to write song-ish poems that simply have no specific meaning to me. I like dreams, I like nightmares, and sometimes life is a scary road to travel.

Goodnight, Farewell

Eyes feel heavy
Mind is racing
Dreams are crashing
Wishes fading
Depression begins to take over.
Push it away,
But it won't budge.
The smile is fading
Harder to show.
Will it win? I don't know.

My heart weeps.
My soul cries.
My hope dies.
My wishes fade away.
I long for the end of the day...

Good night good morning
I have to leave you now
The demons are close
I'm with them now
Goodbye
Farewell
I'll be back again tomorrow.

I'm on a downward spiral
Into the abyss
It's dark inside
Do you miss me yet?
I'm giving into the darkness
Letting the monster take control
Will I ever again feel whole?

My heart weeps.
My soul cries.

My hope dies.
My wishes fade away.
I long for the end of the day...

Good night good morning
I have to leave you now
The demons are close
I'm with them now
Goodbye
Farewell
I'll be back again tomorrow.

Life is a joke
But I can no longer laugh
The punchline is my pain.
I am losing me again.
The darkness is my savior,
I feel safety and comfort there
No longer aware.
Is this my despair?

My heart weeps.
My soul cries.
My hope dies.
My wishes fade away.
I long for the end of the day...

Good night good morning
I have to leave you now
The demons are close
I'm with them now
Goodbye
Farewell
I'll be back again tomorrow.

About *Goodnight, Farewell*

There are a lot of repeated parts in this one. I feel like this added to the understanding of how depression works. It's a daily struggle, even on the good days. Plus, it can come out of nowhere and ruin your entire day. That's also why it found itself in the midst of the happier poems, where I found myself, but the depression still comes back, because that's how it works.

Crashing And Burning

How often do you feel
Like you're falling, falling?
The ladder is gone
And the ground is calling.
There is no rescue.
There is no one around.
What help was there
Has come and gone,
They've left you all alone.
(You're never really alone,
You are your best company)

When it feels as though
You've nowhere else to go,
All hope is gone
And you just want to pass out on the lawn.
(Now is the most important time,
And these things will help you survive.
This to shall pass.
You are not made of glass)
Don't give up
Don't give in
It's all part of the world we live in.

How often do you feel
As though you're climbing, climbing?
It means you made it!
That blood under your fingers?
It means you nailed it!
You survived this thing called life.
You got through this round of strife.
You fight to survive,
And you're still alive.
(You're stronger than you know,
No blizzard can hold you back)

When it feels as though all hope is lost
You're worried about the cost,
You'll realize life will still prevail.
(You may put your heart in jail,
Or cry yourself to sleep at night,
But you will continue to win the fight
Each and every day)
There is always hope,
You've made it up that slope.
You didn't give up.
You didn't give in.
And that is the only way in this life to win.

About *Crashing And Burning*

When I originally wrote this poem it was much shorter. In fact, here is a look at the original.

Crash and Burn

Falling, falling...
The ladder is gone
There is no rescue
It's come and gone.
How do you live?
How do you go on...
When it feels as though
All hope is gone.
Climbing, climbing
Blood under nails
The fight to survive
Is all that prevails.

I feel like the rewrite has turned the poem into something more inspirational than what the original was. It was originally trying to inspire strength in those suffering, but it fell short (pun intended).

I am not sure what the original was written in regards to. It was while I was in a downward spiral of a relationship with that guy I married and later divorced. It probably had some basis in the pain I suffered for years in that relationship, but I could always somehow see that silver lining.

Reaching Toward The Abyss

Panic sets in.
Positivity tries to peak through.
It isn't working.
It's too far gone.
There is too much proof
To believe otherwise.
Panic wins.

Because..
Deceptive virtues keep plaguing my mind
Why is peace so hard to find?
Within my soul, I long to be well
But continually I am just lost in hell

Where...
There is no love
Push always comes to shove
My dreams keep on crashing
Bright lights keep on flashing

This roller coaster ride is never ending
Breaks are jammed
The future is bleak
Something real is all I seek
Maybe the end.
Or a new beginning...

Please...
Don't lie
You won't miss me
When I reach the abyss
Steadily sinking
It's getting darker
I hear the end hearken
No light at the end

No visions to defend
Just the dark
Just the death.

About *Reaching Toward The Abyss*

Sometimes my poetry comes out in my darkest of moments. This was one of them. As someone suffering from anxiety issues of all kinds, including diagnosed social anxiety, I often find it hard to relate to people. It's in that inability to feel human that I get lost and feel like no one cares about me or understands me. It's painful, and you know that if you've ever suffered anxiety or depression. The poetry always reminds me that, if nothing else, I have creativity and the world deserves to have me here sharing my ability (and, hopefully, helping other people realize that death is not the answer).

My Fairy Tale

Once upon a time
I dreamed a lover so true
Before I knew there was you
I hoped and prayed
That I'd make it through each today.

I can be alone
But alone doesn't make a home
And I wanted someone who
I could give my heart to
That would actually cherish it this time.

I longed for
Arms to crawl into
Sweet words whispered
In my ears
Someone to help cast away my fears
Chasing dreams we shared
Our souls bared.

He needed strength to hold me
An ability to calm my fear
And to dry my tears
And you turned that dream
Into a dream come true
And I could never stop feeling this love for you.

Wishes are worth it
When you finally have the right one come true
So wish upon a star
And dream of fairy tales
Know that your happily ever after
Is still out there somewhere.

About *My Fairy Tale*

This poem originally began much the same way as what you just read. However, it originally went to a very dark place where no love existed. I had a rough time last year. I went from one bad relationship to another, and another, both romantically and platonically. Everything seemed to be cast with clouds and shadows and I couldn't see finding true love being something that would ever happen to me. And then it did. So, instead of keeping this poem on the dark side, I rewrote it to show that good things can happen, if you just keep looking and hoping!

What Is This Sleep You Speak Of?

Insomnia comes every time
I'm here alone, I can't let go
So many thoughts in my head
My soul filled with dread
What will tomorrow bring?
Will my soul continue to sing?

Will it all fall apart?
I try to pinpoint the start
When did I get so lost?
What will be the final cost?
It controls my every thought
Leaving my mind feeling wrought

From what will be,
To how I see
It's like I'm the puppet of my feelings
Anxiety controls the strings.
Will I sleep before he sings?
The sound of voices my thought brings,
They aren't mine
And I don't feel fine.

These voices speaking in my head:
One is the voice of the dead.
She's no longer here,
But she still makes me fear.
And the other was a broken heart,
A lost game from its very stay.

How did I get so behind,
And where is the path, I cannot find?
I'm simply broken apart,
Missing so many pieces, where would I start?
No way to put me back together again.

My anxiety will always win.

About *What Is This Sleep You Speak Of?*

When I first started on my path to healing after restarting my life from scratch a few times in one year, I found that my anxiety had complete control over all of my thoughts and actions. On a weekly basis, I was having a mental breakdown, or two. This poem is about that time.

I managed to make it through those tests, and I feel like it has allowed me to be an, even more, understanding person, as well as building on my strength more. I am a survivor.

Where Am I Going?

I've been on a path to nowhere.
I was tired of just going anywhere.
No longer just blowing in the breeze,
Docking my boat from its time on the seas.
It was a path that had no ending,
One that was failing from the beginning.
The rocky road has tossed me around
But I never wanted to be a square
So I lost myself trying to be what someone else wanted,
Not anything like what I needed.
So I finally got the courage to ask the question:
Where am I going?

This new path I've found
Was one I once lost.
It's a return to where I once lived,
Going back in time to begin again from the dead.
Walking away to find me,
No longer concerned about any of you.
I've finally learned your opinions don't count,
I am no longer interested in the numbers.

I've found where happiness waits,
It was never really gone,
It was inside me all along.
I just fell short
Of seeing the path was in me.
You deal with you.
Where am I going?
I've found a place to stay,
I no longer need to roam
Because I found a home.
I found myself,
And I found someone
That makes me not need to search anymore,

Because I am no less.

About *Where Am I Going?*

I wrote this poem right after I left my old life behind. It was originally a little bit different than it is now, and a little shorter. Since I've found myself now, I edited it up a bit. Just know, you can go anywhere you want to go, you just need to get moving!

This one also delves into the fact that I often spend too much time caring what other people think of me. That's something I am working on. If people don't like you the way you are, look for people that do (unless you're a bad person, of course).

You

I wonder if you're a dream...
And I fear to wake each morning
To find you are no longer here.
What would I do if I lost you?
It's something I don't want to think about,
But I can never get it from my mind.

If I lost you
I would probably shout.
What I would say would depend
On what happened to you.
If you were just a dream
I'd rather keep sleeping and never wake again.

If I only dreamed you up,
It's the best dream I've ever had
I'd sleep as much as I could
To find out if it all turns out good,
Or if a nightmare is what I'd find.
Would I still want you then?

Could you ever be real?
When I wake up by your side
I know you're really real
And I cannot hide
The love I feel for you.
But when I sleep alone...

I worry every night,
Afraid to go to sleep
Knowing when I wake alone
I'll wonder if you're real again, or
I'll wonder if you're really gone
Even though you'll always be there.

About *You*

When you start a fresh new relationship and you get past the getting to know each other phase into the "this could be love phase" things can start to get dicey, emotion wise anyway. I wrote this poem a few months into my most recent (and most real) relationship, but after we said: "I love you." It expresses the fear you can feel when you're really connected with someone and you suffer from anxiety.

When I was with him I was comfortable, happy, content. When I would get home I'd be fine until I had to sleep alone, and then the demons would creep into my mind. This phase didn't last too long, though, but long enough to inspire a poem!

You're The Sign

The signs, I've seen them
Every time I look around
Every time I hear the sound
Of your voice, behind me or beside me
You never lead
You're always just there, helping me succeed

These signs include:
A smile from you
Your gentle touch
The way you cuddle me so much
Your helping hand
The way you stand by my side
The love for me you cannot hide

I see them every single day
I'd notice the lack if you went away
I hear it in your voice
You have made a choice
To be my knight in shining armor
To be my light in the harbor

Your smile is my beacon
The light that guides me home
Your hand is my stability
But you'll never be my crutch
I am able to stand without you
But that's something I won't do
Because when I'm with you
The signs say it's true

These signs include:
A smile from you
Your gentle touch
The way you cuddle me so much

Your helping hand
The way you stand by my side
The love for me you cannot hide

About *You're The Sign*

This poem was written in a car (it's OK, I wasn't driving). It was inspired by the great guy that was sitting by my side (and the one doing the driving) and a hawk I saw soaring in the sky. The hawk reminded me of my love for signs, and how this awesome guy has been the biggest sign in my life, that things can always get better. I'll be keeping my eyes out for more signs again in the future, it's a passion I should never have let go of.

Longing For Those Words

We've known each other oh so long
Met up once upon a time over a song
Or a band, maybe a story
Back in our younger glory

Then again fate brought us together
Weeks gone by and I would leave you never
Funny how these feelings grow
Through the ebb and tide, we row
I know exactly how I feel for you
And I know that you feel it too
(It's been on the tips of our tongues
Since we went out on date one)

But I'm longing for those words
Those three we've not said yet
If I was forced to bet
I'd break my will and say them first
But in the past, that's been the worst
(Nothing stings more than unrequited love)

For you to say those three words to me
Proof this is true love, it would be
But yet, I'm longing for those words
... That you have not said

I love you
I love you
But I won't say it yet

Though, every time I look in your eyes
I feel myself come alive
Everything about you makes me happy to breath
I wonder if you can see
How good you are for me

One touch of your hand
Sets my soul on fire
One look from you makes my heart skip a beat
I wonder if you feel it too
Every single time I look at you

About *Longing For Those Words*

Love, infatuation or full-blown passion, can definitely inspire poetry. I usually see this kind of poetry as cheesy or sappy and do my best not to share it. However, in the context of this poetry book, it helps to show that life can go on after divorce, and you can find love again even after you've lost it.

I wrote this one before the man this book is dedicated to said "I love you" for the first time. It was coming, it was always on the verge, and it's the truest love I've ever known.

Off Track

Follow the yellow brick road they said
It will help you find your way
But boy has this path lead me astray
I feel like I've taken the path less chosen
And the only difference it's made is that I am more alone.

Sometimes I love that feeling of loneliness
It reminds me that I can actually feel
It's a catalyst to get the creative juices flowing
Artwork pouring out in words
My thoughts are my therapy.

Do all creatives go through this?
Is being off track the way to success?
But I wish someone could see me
Inside my head, I'm lost
Trying so hard to be something.

Some days it feels like a tornado has swept me
And I am spinning in its funnel
I can't get out and I'm feeling dizzy
But then all is silent
And I can't think or do a thing.

I just want to pick the right path
To climb down the hole or run
This is not a game of hide and seek
My map to the road has been lost
There is no white rabbit.

You can wish for a life manual all you want
But you'll never understand it
It's just a matter of surviving as long as you can
And picking the right people to walk the path with you

Ones that use their hearts, souls, and minds.

About *Off Track*

Off Track is a poem I originally published in an added chapter in the second edition of my dark poetry book, *Dreams of Darkness*. I published it in 2011. It was a much shorter poem, and I decided to lengthen it and give it even more of an Alice and Dorothy theme, as it originally only tied to one with the "there is no white rabbit" part, and that was also originally the last line of the poem.

This poem could be about many things, and since it's an oldie, I think I'll leave it up to your interpretation.

Alone

Alone
You've felt it
I know you have
Everyone feels it

No one is there
No one will listen
No one even cares

You feel trapped in a box
With no way out
Hoping the end is near
There is no doubt
You live in fear

Of being alone
It's not a time of peace for some
You wait for death to come
Because the silence is just too much

No one is there
No one will listen
No one even cares

Even when someone is near
You feel alone
More so than when you're really alone
There's no comfort to behold
And no hope left

You're simply alone
Until the bitter end
Everyone dies alone
And you're still wishing for death

No one is there
No one will listen
No one even cares

About *Alone*

This is another poem from the second edition of *Dreams of Darkness*. Again, since it's an old poem it's really hard to know what the original version was really about. However, with some additions to fill it out, I feel like it explains something we all feel from time to time. Life can be lonely, and loneliness can be really difficult to deal with (even for the happiest people).

I cherish my alone time, but there are times when I'd rather not be alone.

It's Over Now

No future, just past
Past pain, past sorrow
Mistakes we never learn from
Never learning not to make mistakes
The rock rolled over on top of me
And now I am trapped beneath
Warm and flat, dull
Dull like the ache in my heart
A heart I lost
Move on, push past it
"Life goes on," I say
As tears roll down my cheeks
Won't say goodbye
Just walk away
It hurts less that way
It hurts less to hate
Let anger consume
Hurts less on the outside
While it hurts more within
Where no one can see
Won't let anyone in
Never again
I've said this before
I think I have
Like a broken record
The needle's worn thing
Like my endurance for pain
When It's love I thought I was in
Only hurtful moments
To take up some days
Until, now, I'm lonely again
Never wanted to be this way
But the fates say it is so
It's time to let go
And stop fighting

A never ending battle
I just can't win
Only more sorrow within
If I were to wait it out
As it gets worse and worse
Never better like we say
We want it to be that way
Perfect and happy
But I don't think those are real
Not anymore
Not now, not again
I have lost my will to win
My drive to fight
My heart split again
Was it ever whole
Not since I can remember
And I have no soul
Must be why it's over
No soul, no soul mate
Just a big pool of hate
That I can't shake
No blame
Just time to walk away.

About *It's Over Now*

The honest truth is, sometimes you look back at old poems and you don't want to remember what or who they were about. This is one of those. The relationship I had with my ex-husband was one that started way back when I was a teenager, and it was doomed from the start. However, love makes us blind.

This was the final poem I rescued from that old poetry book of mine. I only did some very minor edits to this one, so it is pretty much as close to the original as it could be, without the grammar errors.

Relationships end, and sometimes it's a good thing. I have a tendency to stick around too long in bad relationships (friendships included). I also have a problem in saying "goodbye." It's not nice to just walk away from someone and not explain to them why you're leaving, but sometimes it's the only option. And, sometimes, you do explain yourself and they just don't listen.

June Six Twenty-Fourteen

You left me
I should have been happy you were gone
I didn't get to say goodbye
Maybe that's why
You still haunt me every day
You've been gone for years
But for you, I still shed tears

I wonder why you weren't my friend
Not until toward the end
Moms and daughters have a special bond
We didn't have that all along
You were my captor
I was your slave
You hit me to make me obey
You called me names
There were so many
Quitter, liar, stupid
You tore me down instead of pulling me up
You weren't a mom,
You were simply my abuser

Are you the reason I can't make friends?
Narcissists find me an easy target
Am I look for a replacement for you
I tried to love you, mom
But you broke my heart into pieces

Now you're gone
Each day I wish you were here
Still hearing your voice ringing in my head
Nothing was ever good enough for you,
Nothing I ever did.
Were you proud of me at all?
I thrived and survived despite your gall.

All you did was push me away
A little child needing her mother's love
But when I wanted a goodnight kiss
Instead, I got a shove
When I wanted to feel your embrace
You'd slap me in my face
When I wanted your pride
Instead, I had to hide
From both your hurtful hands
And all of those hateful words.

Why do I still miss you?
Why do you haunt my dreams?
I'm still looking for your approval
The only way for the removal
Of this depression that plagues me
Thoughts of you tearing me apart at the seams
You died too young
You wanted to die
You continued to tell lie after lie
Someone said you were proud of me
Why is it I couldn't see
And why couldn't you just say it to me?

No words I say can end this
An emptiness I now live with
They say the good die young
But sixty-three isn't old
And you were far from good
I never got a chance to stand up to you
You never got your own chances
Like seeing me make the right decisions
The new life I have now, full of revisions
And yours is just over.

About *June Six Twenty-Fourteen*

That was the day my mom died. This poem is about her, my attempt at finally letting go and moving on (but I still don't know if it worked). I carry so much pain and anger with me. My mom was both physically and mentally abusive to me into my teen years, until I moved out of her house. But later in life she sometimes, almost, felt like a friend. I feel like she was really only trying to buy back the love she destroyed while raising me. She had wonderful things to say about anyone that wasn't part of her family. She had nothing nice or kind to say to me, ever. She died too young, at the age of 63, after battling a long illness. She wanted to die. And now I miss her like I lost my best friend. Some days I am mad at her, for being less than the mom I deserved (that any child deserves). Sometimes I'm mad at her for leaving so early. And other times I just want her to be here so I can hug her, talk to her on the phone, and tell her about all of the good choices I have finally been making in my life... Maybe now she'd be proud of me. I still remember all of the terrible things, but I try to find some good in there as well. Rest in peace, mom, so I can go through the rest of my life without you haunting me.

Afterword

While I read through and did the edits on this work of poetry I realized a few things. Pain can often bring out our negative side, so it's important to find a way to heal. There are some things said in the explanations of my poems that may seem harsh, but they are no harsher or mean that the things said about me or done to me by the people they are about. I could have described things differently, but then I feel like it would have made my words less authentic. The point of this collection of poetry is to help, not hurt. I wanted you to understand that many people go through breakups (of relationships and friendships), that many people suffer from anxiety and depression, that many people struggle when they find love, and that many people have family issues.

Please be kind to each other, even the people you don't know. You never know what someone has gone through in their life, and smiles are often used for covering up pain and loneliness.

About The Author

Yvonne was born, but not raised, in Grand Rapids, Michigan. She grew up in a small beach town in the thumb, Harbor Beach. However, Grand Rapids would call her back to its arms (or clutches) a couple times, and now that's where she stays.

Yvonne has been writing poetry since first grade when she "published" her first poetry book (it was hand illustrated and colored, and covered with cardboard with material glued to it, with a hand stitched binding). In 2011 Yvonne self-published a dark poetry book. This one could be considered dark to some people. As a survivor of abuse and someone that suffers from depression and anxiety, Yvonne wanted to share her own personal poetry, her version of a diary, with others in hopes that her words could help and encourage them. There is always a light at the end of the tunnel.

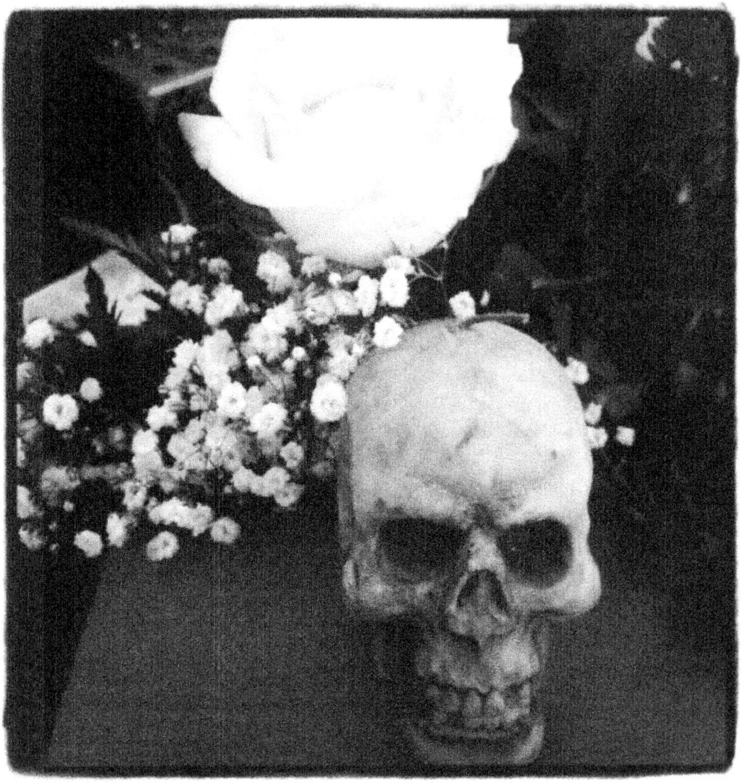

CPSIA information can be obtained
at www.ICGtesting.com
Printed in the USA
LVOW03s1427220517
535408LV00006B/970/P